COPING WITH GENDER FLUIDITY

Stephanie Lundquist-Arora

New York

For Liam and all others with the courage to be themselves

Published in 2020 by The Rosen Publishing Group, Inc.
29 East 21st Street, New York, NY 10010

First Edition

Library of Congress Cataloging-in-Publication Data

Names: Lundquist-Arora, Stephanie, author.
Title: Coping with gender fluidity / Stephanie Lundquist-Arora.
Description: First edition. | New York : Rosen Publishing, 2020. | Series: Coping | Includes bibliographical references and index.
Identifiers: LCCN 2019009354| ISBN 9781725341265 (library bound) | ISBN 9781725341258 (pbk.)
Subjects: LCSH: Gender nonconformity—Juvenile literature. | Gender identity—Juvenile literature.
Classification: LCC HQ77.9 .L86 2020 | DDC 306.76/8—dc23
LC record available at https://lccn.loc.gov/2019009354

Manufactured in China

On the cover: The concept of gender has moved beyond the binary "man" or "woman" categories. Rather, gender identities exist on a multidimensional and evolving continuum.

CONTENTS

INTRODUCTION

Gender identification is gaining more attention as an increasing number of teens identify as nonbinary or genderqueer, meaning outside the traditional binary of male and female. This boost is attributed to the growing comfort level teens have with self-expression, despite societal gender norms. One such example is Jaden Smith, the American rapper, actor, and son of Will Smith and Jada Pinkett-Smith. Smith is not shy in expressing his gender nonconformity. He went to his high school prom in a dress and modeled women's clothing for a Louis Vuitton campaign.

The media and entertainment industries also embrace the gender-fluidity representation. Fictional characters express their nonbinary gender identities in books, movies, and television shows. Real-life role models—such as American entertainer Miley Cyrus, Australian entertainer Ruby Rose, British actor Tilda Swinton, British musician Pete Townshend, Brazilian model Lea T, and Canadian author Rae Spoon—share their personal experiences and expressions in news stories, social media posts, and interviews.

Nonbinary gender identification has existed throughout history and around the world. The *hijra* community in India, which is made up of individuals who do not identify as male or female, dates back to the second century. India officially recognized hijra as a third gender in 2014. Similarly, the *travesti* in Latin America are viewed as people who are concurrently men and women and are also considered to be a third gender. The *waria* of Indonesia are assigned male at birth and grow to experience life as women. Variations of the "two-spirit" people, those with a masculine and a feminine spirit, have been documented in Siberia, New Zealand, the Democratic Republic of the Congo, and among the Navajo Nation in the American Southwest. Fast-forwarding to the twenty-first century, Canada has committed to adding a third "non-binary" gender option to its 2021 census to be more inclusive of its gender-fluid citizens.

Despite the long history of nonbinary gender identification and modern-day awareness, matters of gender identity remain contentious and oversimplified. Some have claimed that the media has reduced transgender rights activism to nongendered bathrooms and locker rooms. Public policies surrounding fair bathroom use has stirred up transphobic rhetoric among segments of the population and do not automatically equate to fair treatment. While some American states have passed

Tilda Swinton, who identifies as gender-fluid, is one of many entertainers who publicly embrace a nonbinary gender identity.

equal access laws, there are some that have not. In addition, gender nonbinary teens are still more likely to attempt suicide and/or experience isolation, bullying, low self-esteem, homelessness, gender dysphoria, and depression than their cisgender (those who have the same internal sense of gender as the gender they were assigned at birth) counterparts. Despite the many challenges, there are many ways to cope with gender fluidity when embarking on and supporting the gender-exploration journey.

CHAPTER ONE

What Is Gender Fluidity?

"Gender-fluid" describes a person who floats between the masculine and feminine ends of the continuum, either slowly over time or at any given point, depending on individual, social, and/or cultural preferences. The term first appeared in the 1980s and is used to describe a nonbinary gender that does not simply check off a "male" box or "female" box. Rather, gender fluidity is a continuum with multiple dimensions, as if drawing a line to connect the boxes.

There is limited data on how many teens identify as gender-fluid. A study published in March 2018 in the journal *Pediatrics* suggests that nearly 3 percent of the respondents identified as "transgender, genderqueer, gender-fluid or unsure of your gender identification." This was an increase

Gender-fluid people float between the masculine and feminine ends of the gender continuum. Gender presentation might fluctuate on a daily basis.

from the 0.7 percent identifying as transgender, as noted in a UCLA study conducted the year prior. The 2015 US Transgender Survey, by the National Center for Transgender Equality, reports that at least 25 to 35 percent of the transgender population identifies as a nonbinary gender. This includes bigender (those with two genders), gender-fluid, genderqueer, and agender (those with no gender).

The Meaning of Gender

In the mid-twentieth century, many people believed that your role, appearance, and behavior were determined largely by your gender assignment at birth. Ideas of gender almost exclusively supported a cisgender world. If you were female, you identified as a woman and presented yourself in feminine ways. A woman was expected to marry a man, wear dresses and pearls, raise children, cook meals for her family, and tend to the needs of the home. If you were male, you identified as a man and presented yourself in masculine ways. You were expected to earn money to support the family, wear suits, and enjoy sports and hunting. Even though gender fluidity existed during this time, it was not culturally supported or recognized among the general population.

Over time, especially with the rise of the second wave of feminism in the latter half of the twentieth century, voices grew louder in objection to the rigid, unfair, and inaccurate view of gender. Feminist scholars such as Betty Friedan and Simone de Beauvoir focused on the expected roles of women in society, noting that women were just as capable outside of the home as men. Similarly, men were capable of cooking, cleaning, and caring for a family inside the home. This new point of view began to revolutionize the way people defined "woman" and "man."

A third wave of feminist thinking came in the 1990s, which shifted away from the binary classification of gender in favor of a broader

In the 1950s, gender roles (as illustrated in this image) were assigned based on gender assignments at birth. Gender fluidity existed at this time, but it was not culturally supported.

conceptualization. Gender theory scholar Judith Butler argued that gender is independent of biological sex. She writes in her book *Gender Trouble: Feminism and the Subversion of Identity* that "*man* and *masculine* might just as easily signify a female body as a male one, and *woman* and *feminine* a male body as easily as a female one." This school of thought challenged socially assigned binary gender categories and provided an opportunity to explore internal and psychological gender identities.

Context Influences Identity

Our identity is shaped by many factors, such as culture, community, ethnicity, birth assignment, genetics, and religion. It is also influenced by what we learn at school, read on the internet, and absorb from our friends. Many of these factors can be static or change over time, causing our identity to be contextual and fluid. For example, you might identify as Californian if you are within the United States or American if you are traveling abroad to Spain. You might think more about what it means to be an American when away from home and pick up new language and customs that alter the way you communicate or behave. You might even consider how being abroad brings out your "American-ness," but minimizes it upon your return home. Similar identity influencers might apply if you are born in Canada with Indian parents. Your Indian background might be more salient when you are around people with other identities. You might eat *dal* and *roti* at home but a turkey and cheese sandwich in the school cafeteria. Or you might feel one way when watching a Bollywood movie with

During World War II, women, like the one featured in the airplane factory advertisement below, were asked to keep the factories running while their male counterparts were off fighting.

family at home but have a different experience when watching it with your non-Indian friends at a movie theater.

Social Construction and the Fluidity of Gender

Sociopolitical and cultural context are also important in gender identity. Think about what it meant to be a woman living in the United States during World War II. Rosie the Riveter was a national symbol for women entering the workplace at a time when most men were off to battle.

Women found themselves in a position where their country needed them to do something that was previously perceived to be a masculine responsibility—to keep the factories running.

On the other hand, consider what it meant to be a woman living in Romania during the 1970s and 1980s. Under the rule of Communist dictator Nicolae Ceausescu, dutiful citizens were expected to have as many babies as possible to help reach

Nicolae Ceausescu, pictured here with his wife and many children in traditional dress, sought to greatly multiply the Romanian population.

his goal of twenty-five million Romanians. Members of the Communist Party entered Romanian factories and workplaces, urging women of childbearing ages to go home and have more children. The role of women in that particular context was to become a baby machine, emphasizing that expectations on gender roles are influenced by biology, but also geographic, sociopolitical, and economic needs. It further implies that gender is a social construct and that ideas about the meaning of gender change, depending on what is happening in the world around us.

In fact, gender is a fluid social construct. Simone de Beauvoir is often cited for the phrase "one is not born, but rather becomes a woman." Judith Butler builds on de Beauvoir's point to lay the theoretical framework for gender fluidity by writing in *Gender Trouble* that gender identity is "a constructing that cannot rightfully be said to originate or end."

Gender-fluid persons are puzzled by attempts made to identify them in static terms on the gender continuum. Six-year-old Tony, assigned male at birth, views gender differently depending on the situation. Tony gets mad if his brother, Marklin, refers to Tony as a sister, but he accepts that the neighbors across the street refer to him as a girl. For some gender-fluid persons, feelings of masculinity and femininity change from day to day and do not depend on their relationships with others. For instance, the *Guardian*

Racial Fluidity

Rachel Dolezal was a civil rights leader, president of a local chapter of the National Association for the Advancement of Colored People (NAACP), and an African American studies university instructor in Spokane, Washington. She identified herself

Rachel Dolezal, former president of a local chapter of the NAACP, brought media attention to the concept of racial fluidity.

as African American, but in June 2015, Dolezal's Caucasian biological parents made a public statement that she was Caucasian. As a result, Dolezal lost her position as NAACP president and many of her friends refused to speak to her. After her white heritage was revealed, Dolezal continued to maintain a black identity. According to Chris McGreal's article in the *Guardian*, she says, "For me, how I feel is more powerful than how I was born. I mean that not in the sense of having some easy way out. This has been a lifelong journey."

The case brought media attention to the concept of racial fluidity. Could Dolezal say she was anything but white? Dolezal had four black adopted siblings. She attended Howard University, a historically black college. She married a black man and was an advocate for civil rights. Many claim that Dolezal's appearance was an offensive impersonation. They suggest that there is a long history of white people claiming to have black heritage when it was convenient. Others claim that race is a social construct and that racial classifications are illogical.

detailed the case of twenty-one-year-old Daniela Esquivel Asturias in 2016. It noted that Daniela feels feminine on some days and prefers to apply lipstick and put on a dress. On other days, Daniela feels masculine and dresses hold no appeal. In the same way that other components of a person's identity are impacted by internal and external factors, gender identification can vary by context.

Gender Fluidity and Boundlessness

As gender fluidity continues to hold a spotlight in the media, many people who do not understand gender identity are confused. Some have a cisgender view of the world and think boys should be masculine and girls should be feminine. They believe gender is a simple fact. In her book, *The Gender Creative Child*, Diane Ehrensaft, who cofounded the Child and Adolescent Gender Center at the University of California, San Francisco, writes, "From those gender creative people who experience it from the inside and those allies who know it from the outside comes an outcry: 'It is not a choice, it is who we are—male, female, or other. It just is.'" With so many variables at play, it is important to recognize the boundless outcomes in gender identity and expressions.

Myths & FACTS

Myth: Gender-fluid people are problems and need to conform to binary constructs of gender.

Fact: To suggest that a gender-fluid individual is problematic is to suggest that someone who is different from you makes them a problem. That is not the case and is considered to be cissexism. On the contrary, people are free to define themselves.

Myth: Gender-fluid is the same as transgender.

Fact: Transgender people identify their gender as something other than their assigned birth gender. Gender-fluid people flow between the masculine and feminine "poles" of gender. There could be some overlap. For instance, a child who was assigned female at birth could slowly realize a male identity, or a child who was assigned male at birth could slowly realize a postgender identity.

Myth: Gender fluidity is the same as sexual fluidity.

Fact: Sexual fluidity is a change in sexual orientation or desire, while sexual orientation has the potential to change with gender identity. For example, a person who is assigned female at birth could fluctuate between the masculine and feminine poles but sexually prefer women.

CHAPTER TWO

The Right to Self-Define

People have a fundamental right to determine who they are, but there tends to be objection when an identity is not a part of mainstream culture. The gender-fluid identity falls into that category, as it is a relatively new concept to mainstream modern culture. It doesn't come with a "best practices manual" and is different for everyone, which makes it especially vulnerable to negative pushback in the media and during public policy debates.

Coming Out to Friends and Family

Sharing your identity with your family and friends can be frightening. It is even scarier if you are afraid

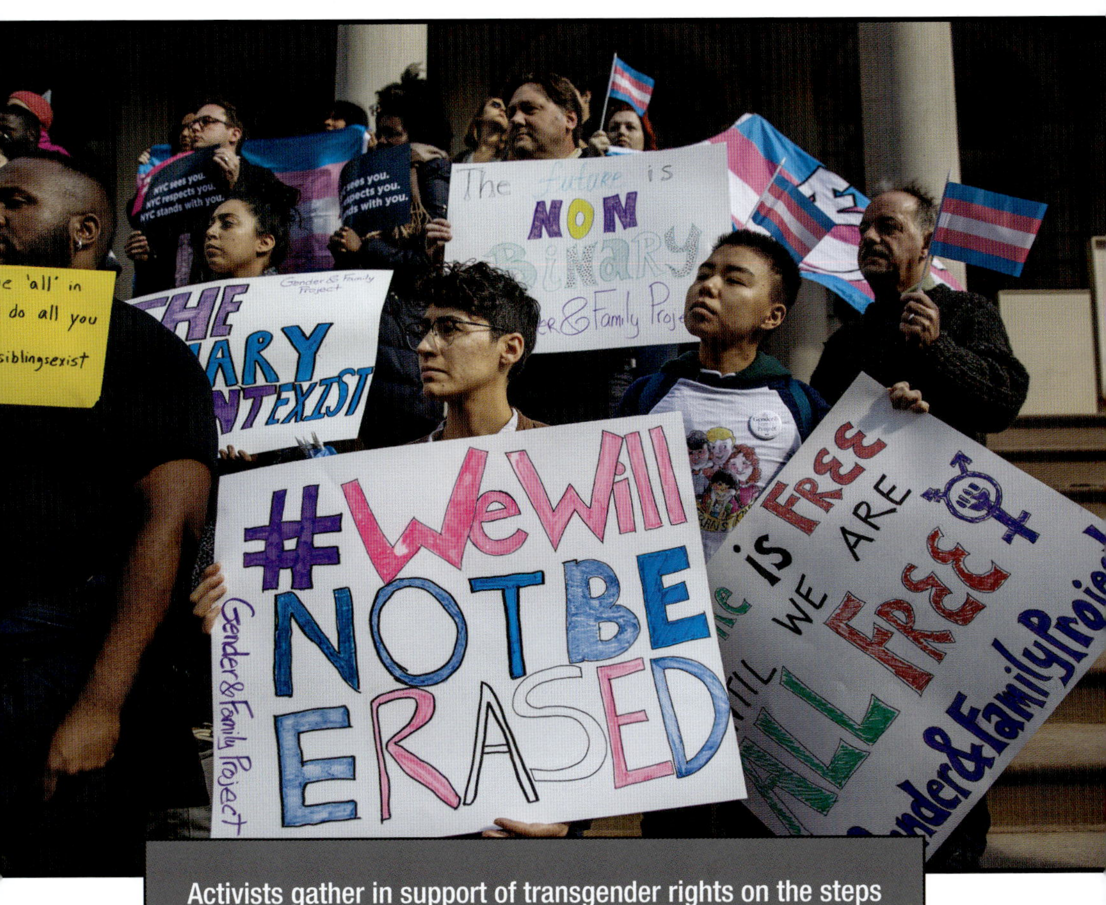

Activists gather in support of transgender rights on the steps of New York City Hall. They lend their voices in an effort to effect change within their community and society at large.

some of them might shun you for being gender-fluid. While it is completely your choice to keep your identity private, many teens find that sharing who they really are with the people they love is very liberating.

Lewis Hancox, a filmmaker, comedy writer, and transgender advocate, explains that coming out

The Matthew Shepard Act

In October 2009, President Barack Obama signed the Matthew Shepard Act into law. The motion expands the 1969 United States Hate-Crime Act to include crimes motivated by a victim's gender, gender identity, sexual orientation, or disability. In 1984, California became the first state to pass hate-crime legislation that included sexual orientation and gender identity.

Matthew Shepard was tortured and murdered because he was gay. The tragedy brought about the inclusion of sexual orientation and gender identity in hate-crime legislation.

At the federal level, the impetus for gender identity and sexual orientation legislative inclusion was a tragic hate-crime committed against twenty-one-year-old Matthew Shepard. He was an openly gay first-year student at the University of Wyoming. On October 6, 1998, after meeting with friends to plan a campus LGBTQ+ (lesbian, gay, bisexual, transgender, and queer or questioning) awareness week, Shepard went to Fireside Lounge bar, where he met Aaron McKinney and Russell Henderson, who pretended to be gay to gain his confidence. The duo lured Shepard to their truck, where they pulled a gun on him, beat him, and took his wallet. They drove him a mile out of town and tied him to a log fence with clothesline. They struck Shepard in the face about twenty times with the gun, took his shoes, and left him to die. About eighteen hours later, in the frigid Wyoming autumn, a teenager on a mountain bike discovered the unconscious, barely breathing Shepard. Five days later, he died in the hospital.

Matthew Shepard's death was devastating, senseless, and tragic—but not in vain. It was the brutal death that woke a nation. Equal rights are not immediate after legislative gains, but it is a critical step in the path to equality. Kim Nash, a member of the local Lesbian, Gay, Bisexual and Trans-gendered Association (LGBTA), summarized it best when she said, "We were the last group it was O.K. to hate. Because of Matthew's death it's a little less O.K."

is different for everyone. According to his article on the website Ditch the Label, he offers these general tips to consider for the coming-out process:

- Come out to yourself first.
- Make connections with others.
- Have a family meeting.
- Have patience for others to absorb the information.
- Consider your name. If you would like a gender-neutral name or one that better reflects your gender identity, you can legally change it.
- If you need to, contact your doctor for questions about puberty blockers or cross-sex hormones.
- Live your life. Embrace all the other aspects of your identity and continue pursuing your dreams.

Everyone's coming-out experience is unique. The important thing to remember is that you are not alone on your journey.

Gender Dysphoria

When society labels people in a way that does not reflect their internal identity, it can be disorienting and confusing. Gender dysphoria is just that, describing the effect caused by a disconnect between a person's internal sense of gender and the one assigned to them. The incongruence can cause stress and anxiety, often resulting in depression. Teens might experience gender dysphoria if they are labeled as one thing but identify as something else, if they want to be a different gender altogether, or when they are unable to express their gender identity because of cultural restrictions.

Not all gender-fluid and transgender people experience gender dysphoria, but many do. According to the National Center for Biotechnology Information, a 2017 school-based survey suggested that 1.3 percent of sixteen- to nineteen-year-olds experienced potentially clinically significant gender dysphoria. In a June 2013 blog article on Tarnished Sophia, the writer uses Shakespeare's *Romeo and Juliet* to describe the discomfort of being mislabeled. The blogger explains:

> *You are meant to play Romeo … Moreover, the person has gone through all the rehearsals as Romeo right up till the day of the first public performance. But when opening night comes, the director hands*

Inclusion in Athletics

Improved self-esteem, better grades, and higher professional and educational goals are just some of the benefits students enjoy when participating in organized school sports. This is especially true for LGBTQ+ students. GLSEN, an educational organization working toward the inclusion of students from kindergarten through twelfth grade, found that LGBTQ+ students reported an increased sense of belonging when they took part in high school sports. In addition, coaches and

Mack Beggs (*center*) took first place at a state wrestling championship in Texas. Transgender and gender-fluid inclusion in school athletics is an important aspect of equality for teens.

teammates can be powerful allies. Liam, a fourteen-year-old transgender teen, started wrestling when he was in fourth grade, two years before he came out. Liam says, "Since I have been wrestling with my coaches since day one, they all have known me for a while. So when I came out they had my back. [They] knew me as a person and a wrestler and wanted to keep me going."

Gender-fluid and transgender inclusion in school athletics is important. In 2016, GLSEN partnered with athletes and advocates to ask LGBTQ youth for ways to include transgender students in athletics. Key suggestions included the following:

- Students can participate in athletics based on their gender identity, regardless of the assigned gender on their birth certificates.
- Transgender eligibility claims should be considered fairly within the district via assistance from a state association.
- The state association should consider eligibility claims by forming a committee of experts familiar with the student's case and transgender athletics.
- Students have a right to privacy and confidentiality during the committee's consideration of eligibility claims.
- Once approved, athletes have access to the same locker rooms and bathrooms as their teammates with the same gender identity.

> *you the script for Juliet. You haven't played this part before, you don't know the lines, the costume doesn't fit at all, and you feel no connection to this character whatsoever. You don't understand what her motivations are, and the director can't explain them in a way that makes any sense to you. But there is no choice. You MUST play Juliet or else everyone will mock you, beat you up, and torment you for years … This is what it's like every single day for someone like myself.*

While there are many resources for treating gender dysphoria, the main objective is to create a sense of harmony among a person's identified gender, body, and self-expression.

The Intersectionality of Race and Gender

The theory of intersectionality makes it clear that multiple components of identity and context work in tandem to shape a person's reality. The term was first coined in 1989 by feminist theorist Kimberlé Crenshaw. She argued that race must be taken into account when discussing gender. Black women, Crenshaw suggests, have an experience

Sojourner Truth, an antislavery and women's rights activist, highlighted the double standard of gender expectations for black and white women in her "Ain't I a Woman?" speech.

that is different from that of both white women and black men, and it cannot be understood by simply scrutinizing the sum experience of both groups. She believes that being black in tandem with being a woman is a unique experience because of its intersection.

Sojourner Truth, a former slave, antislavery campaigner, and women's rights activist, provides a very clear case of intersectionality. In May 1851, at a women's rights meeting in Ohio, Truth delivered the landmark speech "Ain't I a Woman?" In it, she points out the double standard of gender roles and expectations for white women and black women and that their experience could not be more different.

> *That man over there says that women need to be helped into carriages and lifted over ditches, and to have the best place everywhere. Nobody ever helps me into carriages, or over mud puddles, or gives me any best place! And ain't I a woman? ... I have borne thirteen children, and seen most all sold off to slavery, and when I cried out my mother's grief, none but Jesus heard me! And ain't I a woman?*

Intersectionality is particularly relevant for

the transgender and gender-fluid communities. Transgender women of color are at a greater risk of violence than other women, both trans and cisgender, and other people of color, trans and cisgender alike. The Human Rights Campaign published a report in 2018 indicating that at least twenty-two transgender people were killed in the United States in 2018, and eighteen of them (82 percent) were women of color. The same report found that 41 percent of black transgender people experienced homelessness at one time in their lives, a rate that is five times higher than that of the population of the United States.

Gender Expression

While gender identity is how you feel on the inside, gender expression is how you outwardly express your gender identity. Also known as gender presentation, gender expression is very personal and can change at any time, depending on how you feel and your level of comfort. This is especially apparent if a gender-fluid teen opts for a more cisgender expression based on fear of bullying or transphobia. In the *Trans Teen Survival Guide*, authors Owl and Fox Fisher describe gender presentation by saying, "Generally we like to view presentation as a threefold thing, where people can present as feminine, masculine or

Being an androgynous individual means that both feminine and masculine presentations are shown at the same time.

androgynous … while these terms describe a certain presentation, it's important that we realize how fleeting and changing they are."

Gender expressions include your manner of speaking, name choices, type of clothing and color scheme choices, accessories, hair, nails, makeup (or lack thereof), and body appearance. These can be temporary, such as adding jewelry, putting together particular outfits, and binding, padding, or tucking body parts to alter the physical appearance of your body. Binding is a way to appear more masculine by using a wrap to bind the chest for a flat appearance. It should be done properly to avoid injuries, such as rashes, restricted blood flow, and cracked ribs. To express femininity, some people use padding to add curves to their breasts and hips. Those who wish to hide male genitalia rely on a practice called "tucking."

Tucking is done with the help of special undergarments and tools. Conversely, people can give the appearance of having a penis by packing or placing rolled socks or a medical prosthesis in their undergarments. Gender presentation can also be permanent. Some people opt for tatooing, while others choose more invasive procedures such as surgery. These methods can vary greatly among cultures.

Names and Pronouns

Names and pronouns are important, as they signal who we are to the world and how we see ourselves in public and private. Everyone has a right to select what they would like to be called and the pronouns that best reflect their gender identification and presentation. Many gender-fluid people prefer gender-neutral names, such as Alex, Casey, Dakota, Riley, Sidney, or Toni. Others keep or slightly alter the name they were given at birth, like Lewis (formerly Lois) Hancox, referred to earlier in this chapter. If you are interested in changing your legal name—and/or assigned gender—organizations such as the Transgender Law Center in the United States, Mermaids UK, and Trans Equality Canada offer guidance and resources to do it legally and affordably.

While “she” and “he” are the most familiar singular subjective pronouns in mainstream culture, there are many pronouns that can be used to represent gender fluidity. An increasing number of transgender and gender-fluid people prefer the pronoun “they” in the singular form to demonstrate gender neutrality. “Ze” is also a popular choice, as it refers to any gender.

CHAPTER THREE

The Bathroom Battleground

If you watch the news, you might see heated debates about a "bathroom bill." A bathroom bill is the legislation or statute that defines who has access to bathrooms and/or locker rooms and who does not. In some cases, a bathroom bill supports the rights of transgender people to use the facilities designated for their gender identity. In other cases, bathroom bills explicitly ban transgender individuals from using the facilities for their gender and require them to use a bathroom or locker room of the gender they were assigned at birth. Bathroom bills vary by state and school districts.

Federal Regulations for Bathroom Bills

States have to comply with federal regulations, but there is not much in terms of federal guidance.

The New York City Gay Pride Parade is a staging ground for a variety of issues the LGBTQ+ community faces. Discriminatory bathroom bill legislation is among them.

In 2016, the US Department of Education and the US Department of Justice issued a joint statement suggesting that schools have a Title IX obligation to provide transgender students with facilities that are consistent with their gender identity, which the letter defines as "an internal sense of gender [which] may be different from or the same as the person's sex assigned at birth." When the political landscape changed, however, so did the federal government's opinion on transgender rights. In February 2017, the Departments of Education and Justice issued another statement withdrawing the 2016 statement, thereby withdrawing federal government protections for transgender students.

The United States Supreme Court is another institution that has the power to make policy at the federal level, although it has not decided any cases regarding transgender bathroom rights. In March 2017, the Supreme Court decided it would not hear Gavin Grimm's case about a Title IX violation of his rights to use the men's bathroom. Grimm is a transgender man who was refused access to the boy's bathroom at his high school in Gloucester County, Virginia. Rather than deciding the case, the Supreme Court sent it back to a lower court in Virginia. In May 2018, a district court in Virginia ruled that the school had in fact violated Grimm's rights. It was a small victory, but the district court ruling did not have a federal policy consequence as would have been the case if it were adjudicated by the Supreme Court.

The Debate: Facts and Myths

The 2015 National Center for Transgender Equality Survey revealed that 59 percent of transgender

State Bathroom Bill Legislation

On March 23, 2016, after the North Carolina General Assembly passed the Public Facilities Privacy & Security Act, Republican governor Pat McCrory signed it into law. North Carolina had effectively banned transgender people from using the bathroom corresponding to their gender. This act was the first of its kind at the state level to address transgender access to restrooms. Subsequently, many states proposed their own laws, which either required individuals to use the bathroom designated for their assigned gender at birth or, conversely, banned discrimination in public accommodations based on gender identity. States that have proposed (but not necessarily passed) legislation or ballot initiatives threatening equal access to public facilities for transgender people include Alabama, Arkansas, Illinois, Iowa, Kansas, Kentucky, Minnesota, Missouri, Montana, New York, Oklahoma, South Carolina, South Dakota, Tennessee, Texas, Virginia, Washington, and Wyoming.

As of June 2018, the states that have passed legislation protecting the right of transgender people to access restrooms corresponding with their internal gender identities include California, Colorado,

(continued on the next page)

#WeAreNotThis opposes North Carolina's "bathroom bill," which restricted people to using the bathroom based on the sex listed on their birth certificate.

(continued from the previous page)

Connecticut, Delaware, Hawaii, Illinois, Iowa, Maine, Maryland, Massachusetts, Minnesota, Nevada, New Jersey, New Mexico, Oregon, Rhode Island, Vermont, Washington, and Washington, DC. The National Center for Transgender Equality (NCTE) helps the public follow pending legislation and offers ways to participate in legislative efforts to support transgender rights.

people avoided using a public restroom. Of the respondents, 24 percent reported that their presence in a public restroom was questioned or challenged. Opposition to fair bathroom use is generally based on the two myths below, neither of which is supported by empirical evidence:

Myth 1: Transgender people more frequently commit sex crimes in public restrooms and locker rooms.
Fact: In 2018, forensic psychiatrists Brian Barnett, Renee Sorrentino, and Ariana Nesbit found that there has been only one instance in which a transgender person was charged with voyeurism in a public bathroom. In comparison, since 2004, there have been at least 154 cases in the United States of cisgender men who allegedly committed sex crimes in public restrooms. These men did not attempt to disguise their gender nor did they suggest that their presence there was because of trans-inclusive bathroom laws.
Myth 2: Cisgender, straight male sexual predators will pretend they are transgender, or otherwise purposefully abuse fair bathroom laws, to prey on women.
Fact: There was one Seattle-based case in which a man allegedly entered and undressed in a women's

locker room in 2016 because of the Washington State ruling allowing people to choose a bathroom based on internal gender identity. Since 2004, there have been thirteen cases, less than one a year, in the United States in which men have dressed up as women to enter restrooms or locker rooms to commit crimes. That number pales in comparison to the 154 cisgender men who allegedly committed sex crimes in bathrooms and locker rooms during the same time period without concealing their gender identity or mentioning fair bathroom laws.

The empirical data since 2004 suggests that cisgender men are much more likely to be sexual predators in public restrooms and locker rooms than transgender people, regardless of the fair bathroom use laws. There is no evidence to suggest that trans-inclusive public facility laws lead to attacks in restrooms and locker rooms.

Public perception is not always based on data. The Gallup's Values and Beliefs poll conducted in May 2017 found that 48 percent of Americans said that bathroom use should be based on sex assignment at birth, while 45 percent of Americans said bathroom use should be based on gender identity. Seven percent of respondents indicated that they had no opinion. The good news

Transgender Rights in Small Towns

In October 2017, the Grass Lake School Board affirmed a district-wide policy allowing transgender students to use the bathroom corresponding with

(continued on the next page)

The Trevor Project is an organization that helps LGBTQ+ youth cope with suicidal thoughts. Suicidal thoughts and attempts are alarmingly higher among LGBTQ+ teens than their counterparts.

(continued from the previous page)

their gender identity. The decision in the small, conservative community in rural Michigan met with active resistance.

Cruz, a transgender boy in the Grass Lake school district, was at the heart of the debate. Cruz's mom, Terri, explains that when he is able to use the boy's bathroom, he does not say things like, "Everybody hates me" or "I wish I were dead." Terri argues that her advocacy and Cruz's focus on facilities is not obsessive, as some critics claim. She explains in a phone interview with the news site ThinkProgress, "It's not just about a bathroom, just like it was never about drinking fountains during the civil rights movement. [Cruz] feels all of that hatred and discrimination coming at him."

Liam, a transgender boy in the Grass Lake school district, also is able to use the boys' bathroom at school. Liam describes his experience:

> *This year I started using the regular bathrooms and the locker rooms and it was really normal for me and the people in my grade. When I started using the locker room this year my friends had asked me why I used the unisex bathrooms to change*

in and I told them I was not supposed to use the locker room yet because there wasn't protections for me to use it just in case someone wanted to sue, and they responded with "that's stupid" or "so who cares you're not any different."

Liam's mom, Jaimie, an advocate in the debate, further details the heartening support in their community when she explains, "These kids and staff stand up for [Liam] and respect him because of the fact that they have seen this kid since kindergarten and know this is just Liam." Change is often met with resistance and bullying. Young people tend to adapt faster than their parents. Sometimes the most beautiful success stories are found in unexpected places.

for advocates of fair bathroom laws is that the percentage of Americans indicating that bathroom use should be based on gender identity, rather than sex assigned at birth, is increasing over time.

Ban on Transgender People in the Military

The political and media focus on the bathroom bill debates sometimes overshadows the other areas of transgender discrimination. Transgender people are disproportionately unemployed and homeless, and do not enjoy equal access to medical care. They also may not be able to serve in the military, which is an issue that is under much political debate.

On June 30, 2016, Defense Secretary Ashton Carter announced that transgender Americans could serve openly

US Navy sailors cut a cake to celebrate LGBT Pride Month. However, national policies do not always reflect or support equal rights regarding nonbinary expressions and sentiments.

in the military. As part of President Barack Obama's administration, Carter commissioned a study to determine the effects of such a policy. The study was conducted by the RAND Corporation and found that allowing transgender Americans to openly serve "would cost little and have no significant impact on unit readiness." It estimated that 2,450 active-duty members of the military were transgender at the time. Vice President Joseph Biden was also an avid supporter of this policy of inclusion. According to Mara Keisling's article on Medium, Biden stated that transgender rights "were the civil rights issue of our time."

The political landscape changed dramatically in many ways with the election of President Donald Trump. On January 22, 2019, the United States Supreme Court confirmed a Trump administration policy that effectively revived the ban on most transgender people from serving in the military. President Trump announced the initial policy via his Twitter account on July 26, 2017. He wrote that allowing transgender people to serve openly in the military leads to "tremendous medical costs and disruption." According to Adam Liptak's *New York Times* article, lawyers questioned the Trump administration's policy by noting, "The government has presented no evidence that [transgender people serving openly in the military] harms military readiness, effectiveness or lethality." This debate is likely to continue over time as a change in the majority political party may influence the executive and legislative branches of government.

CHAPTER FOUR

To Hormone or Not to Hormone: That Is the Question

Puberty can be a difficult time for everyone, especially for those who are gender-fluid or transgender. People who were assigned female at birth usually go through puberty between the ages of ten and fourteen years old. Those assigned male at birth begin puberty between twelve and sixteen years old. The onset of these physical changes often exacerbates gender dysphoria in transgender or gender-fluid teens because they are moving the body farther from where the mind

Puberty is a difficult and confusing time for everyone, particularly for gender-nonconforming teens. There are many medical and nonmedical options to address gender dysphoria.

thinks it should be and how it should develop. During puberty, gender-fluid teens might experience anxiety, stress, and/or depression. For some gender nonbinary teens, nonmedical gender expressions can be a satisfactory way to present their desired gender identity, but for others it is not enough. There are many medical options to help delay puberty and shape your body to fit your gender identity.

Puberty Blockers and Hormone Replacement Therapy

Gender-fluid youth exploring their gender identities can delay or prevent the onset of puberty to give them more time to reflect how they want their bodies to develop. If a gender-fluid child subsequently decides to identify with the gender assigned at birth, the effects of the puberty-blockers will be reversed when the medication is no longer taken.

Many doctors suggest that the benefits, including alleviating the effects of gender dysphoria, outweigh the potential risks of the medication. Puberty blockers, however, are known to decrease bone density and perhaps lead to an increased likelihood of osteoporosis as the patient ages. Other risks are unknown. Because the brain develops substantially over the course of puberty, doctors are unsure of the specific neurocognitive effects of puberty blockers. While puberty blockers might be helpful and necessary for some people, the decision to take any medication should not be made lightly.

As you continue on your gender identity journey, you might find that you identify with the gender opposite of that which you were assigned at birth. At this point, you might be interested in making more obvious physical changes to your body. With hormone replacement therapy, which is the use of testosterone (the key male sex hormone) or estrogen (the key female sex hormone), most physical changes occur over a two-year period. A female-assigned person who desires a masculine presentation can take testosterone, which will deepen the voice, enhance facial and body hair growth, decrease body fat, enlarge the clitoris, increase the libido (sex drive), put an end to menstruation, and minimize breast tissue.

Hormone replacement therapy, specifically the use of testosterone in this case, has been instrumental in helping Liam, a fourteen-year-old transgender boy, present his desired gender identity and lessen gender dysphoria. Via an email interview for this book, Liam describes his experience, "When I started testosterone I noticed a drop in my voice in about a month … I didn't like my voice because it was higher than most of the boys in my grade. Starting testosterone really helped with dysphoria, because of how it changed the way I am presented." Liam's mother, Jaimie, adds, "Since the day this young man started his testosterone another person emerged. I swear when his voice started to drop, he would talk just to hear his own voice … Every time he starts to see more hair growing he gets very excited. He's so proud of his appearance as it changes."

There are many cases like Liam's, in which a child experiencing incongruence between the assigned gender and actual gender identity seeks hormone replacement therapy and has positive outcomes, such as mental well-being and a better self-image.

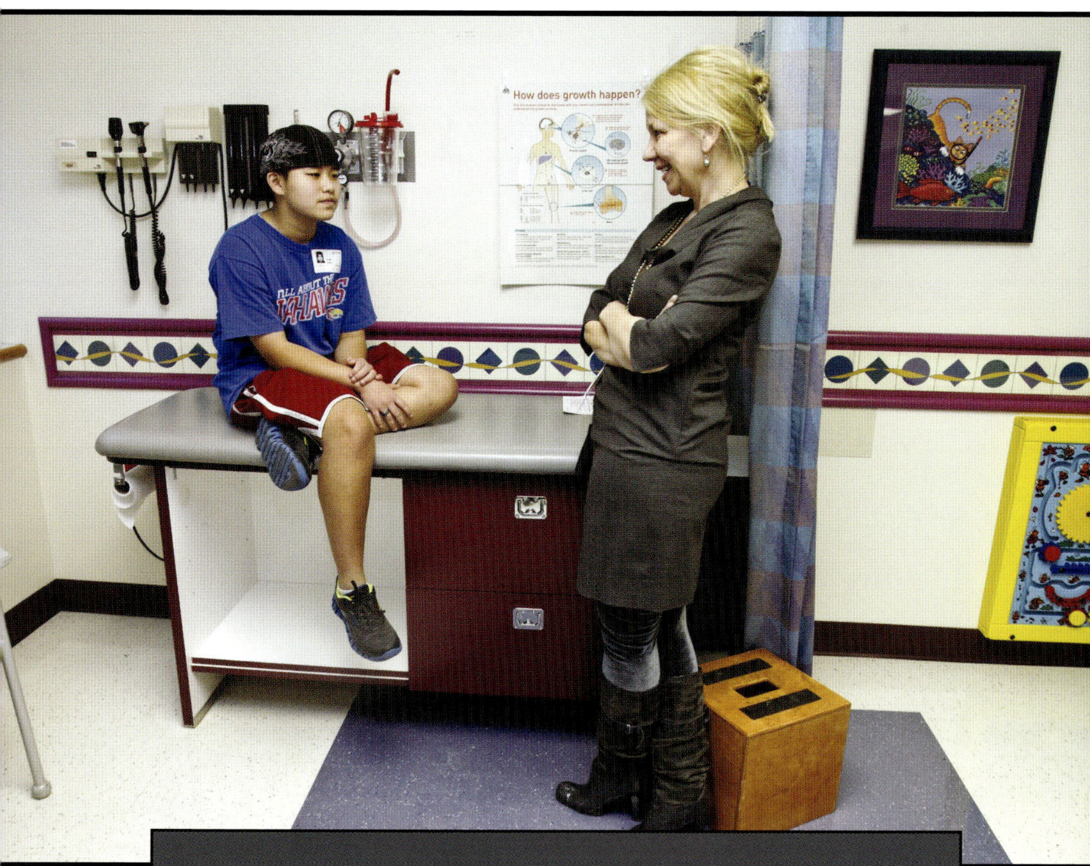

Many teens experiencing gender dysphoria seek hormone replacement therapy, which can result in improved mental well-being and self-image.

Someone assigned male at birth who identifies as female and desires a more feminine presentation might choose to take estrogen as feminizing hormone therapy. This produces breast growth, body fat redistribution, softer skin, decreased hair growth on the face and body, testicular atrophy, the slowing of scalp hair loss, a decreased libido, and fewer spontaneous erections.

There are some risks with the use of testosterone and estrogen. While the degree to which patients experience negative side effects varies, it is important to speak to your doctor about your personal risk factors before undergoing this form of treatment. The Mayo Clinic suggests that complications associated with masculinizing hormone therapy might include infertility, an overproduction of red blood cells, weight gain, acne, male-pattern baldness, sleep apnea, elevated liver function tests, an abnormal amount of lipids in the blood, worsening of psychological conditions, and/or high blood pressure. Meanwhile, the Mayo Clinic explains that complications with feminizing hormone therapy might include infertility, blood clots, weight gain, gallstones, elevated liver function tests, decreased libido, erectile dysfunction, high potassium, high blood pressure, type 2 diabetes, and/or cardiovascular disease.

Process for Youth Treatment at the Gender Management Service Clinic

In 2007, the Gender Management Service (GeMS), an interdisciplinary clinic within Boston Children's Hospital, became the first of its kind in the Western Hemisphere to treat pediatric gender-expansive patients. The clinic now treats patients between the ages of three and twenty-five years old. GeMS takes a team approach to offer gender-affirmative care, partnering with experts from many specialties, including primary care, adolescent medicine, therapy, plastic surgery, reproductive endocrinology, urology, schools and academic institutions, and LGBTQ+ support groups and organizations.

The consultation, assessment, and care processes vary depending on the patient's age. GeMS specifies that its age-specific approaches are as follows:

- For children nine years old and younger: The GeMS-Youth (GeMS-Y) program offers consultations to gender-diverse youth and their families, a play therapy assessment with the child, discussion of specific and general gender issues in young children, and assistance accessing resources in the community.
- For children and teens ages nine to eighteen: GeMS offers an individualized and comprehensive psychological and medical assessment. GeMS typically schedules the first five visits during the first phone call. This is meant to optimize continuity of care and is not intended to be a timeline to intervention. GeMS requires that the patient be in individual therapy, which it will help to facilitate if the child does not have a therapist.
- For young adults over age eighteen: The appointment process is typically shorter than the protocols for younger patients. While GeMS does not require the patient to have an individual therapist, it is encouraged and they will refer you to one.

Surgical Intervention

While some gender-fluid teens will continue to have a fluctuating gender identity as they mature, others will identify more permanently with the gender not assigned to them at birth. In this case, and usually after hormone treatment, they opt for more permanent medical interventions that will produce the results that align with their gender

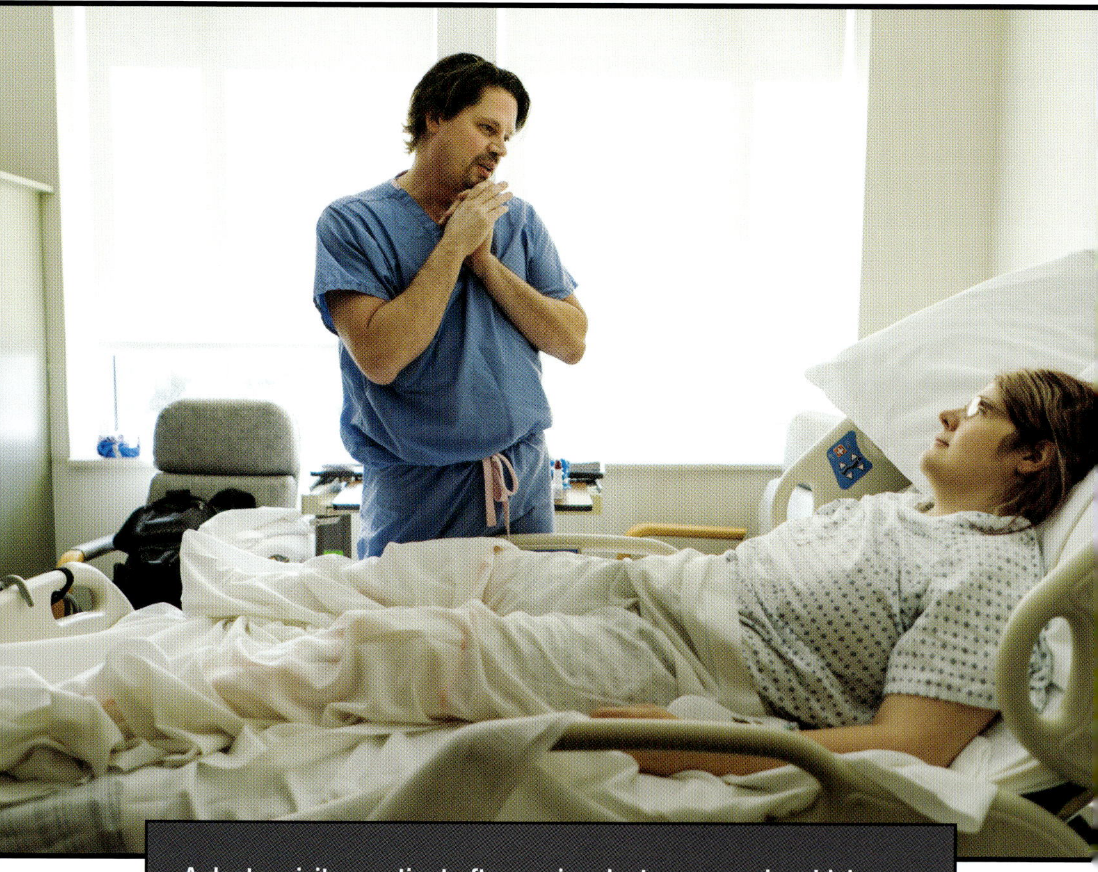

A doctor visits a patient after vaginoplasty surgery, in which a vagina is created from genital tissue. Vaginoplasty surgery is one of many types of gender-affirming surgical options.

presentation and identity. The World Professional Association for Transgender Health (WPATH) recommends that surgical intervention "should not occur until there has been adequate time for adolescents and their parents to assimilate fully the effects of earlier interventions." There are many types of gender-affirming surgeries. People have different preferences in terms of which surgeries make them feel more comfortable with their bodies. These surgical procedures include but are not limited to the following:

- Vaginoplasty: A vagina is created from existing genital tissue.
- Metoidioplasty: A penis is surgically created from existing genital tissue.
- Phalloplasty: A penis and urethra is created from harvested "flap(s)" of skin and other tissues from a donor site on the body, usually the forearm.
- Chest reconstruction: The removal of excess breast tissue to create a more masculine appearance of the chest.
- Breast augmentation: The use of implants to increase the breast size for a more feminine appearance.
- Mastectomy: The surgical removal of the breasts.
- Facial feminization surgery: The modification

of facial characteristics to create a more feminine presentation.

- Vocal surgery: The alteration of the vocal cords to give the voice a higher or lower pitch.

It is important to note that all surgeries have risks and the decision to have surgery should not be made lightly. In the case of irreversible interventions, particularly genital surgery, WPATH recommends that patients should be the legal age of majority in their country—eighteen years old in the United States and Canada—and should have lived for at least twelve continuous months in the gender role that is congruent with their gender identity.

Obstacles to Medical Treatment

There are many barriers to medical care for gender-fluid and transgender people. While insurance denial and lack of financial resources are the most significant among them, negative attitudes and legal barriers can stand in the way of medical care. In the 2015 Transgender Survey, 33 percent of respondents who went to see a doctor within the previous year reported that they had a negative experience based on their gender identity. While many doctors and medical organizations endorse and adhere to guidelines for transgender health care, some do not. It is critical to find doctors who have a gender-affirming approach and are willing to write referrals for specialists.

As a patient, you should not have to educate your doctor on gender dysphoria or persuade them on philosophical matters. When you call the clinic to schedule an appointment, ask questions to determine whether or not the doctor has a gender-affirming approach. For example, ask questions such as, "Do you adhere to the World Professional Association for Transgender Health's Standards of Care?" and "Are you willing to prescribe puberty blockers, cross-sex hormones, or provide specialist referrals for transgender youth?" If the answer is no, look for another doctor.

Age of consent and state health care policy exclusions provide the most substantial legal barriers to care. Parental consent is required for transition-related medical care for patients under the age of eighteen, and while Medicaid programs vary from state to state, most do not cover transition-related health care.

There are many ways to utilize others' expertise on how to access health care. Local transgender communities and LGBTQ+ support groups on social media can provide a wealth of information. The odds are that many of them have experienced the same problems you are facing and can point

Local transgender communities and LGBTQ+ support groups offer a wealth of information regarding access to medical care and wellness resources.

you toward helpful doctors and resources. If you are in the San Francisco area, for example, Trans Thrive (@TransThrive on Facebook) is a nonprofit organization that helps transgender people get access to health care with its resources and drop-in clinic. Canada's *Trans-Health* magazine (trans-health.com) lists organizations in Canada, the United States, and

England that specialize in transgender medical care and support services.

When transgender people are in need of basic medical care unrelated to their gender or transitioning process, fear of discrimination and poor treatment often prevent them from seeing a doctor. Consequently, minor yet treatable problems become cause for emergency room visits. When transgender youth with gender dysphoria cannot access health care, they sometimes rely on "street" hormones, without any medical supervision. These hormones can be very harmful and if administered with a shared needle can put you at risk for human immunodeficiency virus (HIV) and other blood-borne pathogens.

CHAPTER FIVE

Gender Fluidity and Mental Health

The transition from childhood to adulthood is not easy for anyone, regardless of identity. Societal and familial challenges can be catalysts for teenage depression. Gender-fluid teens often face obstacles to mental well-being. They may feel socially isolated and rejected and have little to no self-worth and self-esteem. Some gender-fluid teens inflict self-harm and experience suicidal thoughts and/or attempts. If this describes you, know that you are not alone and immediate help is available.

Gender-fluid and transgender teens often experience feelings of rejection and isolation, but there is a welcoming community that is ready to support them and speak out for their rights.

Institutional Change

While gender fluidity is not new to the world, it is a concept that is relatively new to mainstream culture. The vocabulary (including pronouns), medical and psychological fields, and legal and

Teens perform live at the Trevor Project's TrevorLIVE, a biannual gala, in New York City. The Trevor Project provides 24/7 crisis and suicide intervention for LGBTQ+ youth.

educational systems are all making institutional changes to adapt. One significant breakthrough has been in the psychological conceptualization of gender dysphoria. In 1952, the *Diagnostic and Statistical Manual of Mental Disorders (DSM)* listed gender dysphoria as a mental disorder that could be treated.

Gender Fluidity and Depression

Gender-fluid teens experience higher rates of depression and anxiety than their cisgender counterparts. Gender-variant teens who have not come out are even more likely to experience depression. They are generally concerned about how family and peers will react to their gender identity. When they have not identified publicly, they are more likely to lack support and experience feelings of isolation. In some cases, they attempt suicide when severely depressed.

In 2018, an American Academy of Pediatrics study found that 41.8 percent of nonbinary adolescents had attempted suicide. The Centers for Disease Control and Prevention released a 2019 report indicating that 35 percent of high school students identifying as transgender had attempted suicide within the last year. Therefore, it is crucial for gender nonbinary and transgender teens and their allies to recognize the signs of depression. These can include:

- Sadness, emptiness, or hopelessness
- Anger, irritability, or frustration over normally insignificant things

(continued on page 69)

Depression sometimes leads to self-harm, including cutting with razor blades. Part of being an ally and/or advocate for gender-fluid teens means recognizing signs of depression.

(continued from page 67)

- Little to no sleep
- A change in appetite
- Poor performance and/or attendance at school
- Loss of interest in activities or hobbies, including socialization
- Difficulty making decisions or remembering things
- Drug or alcohol use
- Self-harm
- Suicidal thoughts and/or attempts

If you are experiencing depression or a friend is, there are many resources that can help, including gender and sexual minority–specific crisis helplines. The Trevor Project is one such example, as it provides crisis and suicide intervention for LGBTQ+ people under age twenty-five.

The *DSM* was thereby making the implicit assumption that gender identity disorder was the patient's personal issue, rather than one that resulted from an unaccepting, cisgender society. In 2013, the fifth edition of the American Psychiatric Association's (APA) *Diagnostic and Statistical Manual of Mental Disorders* broadened the concept to highlight the "distress" that the incongruity between one's actual gender and socially assigned gender causes. The APA's definitional change thereby broadened access to care for those experiencing gender dysphoria. Many mental health professionals were already well aware of the distress, but the institutional change encouraged others to follow suit. Consequently, the mental health field began to adopt a gender-affirming approach to gender identity. This marks an important shift in psychology. Research is increasingly showing that when children are supported in affirming their gender identity, their mental health issues decrease, but when they are not supported, mental health difficulties increase.

Bullying

Bullying in school is more frequently due to sexual orientation and gender identity than matters of race, religion, or disability. In a GLSEN survey, students between the ages of thirteen and twenty years old shared their experiences at school. The study found that 90 percent of respondents heard negative remarks regarding gender expression. Further, 56 percent of transgender students responded that they were verbally harassed because of gender expression either "frequently" or "often," with another 18 percent responding "sometimes." Of all the respondents, 32 percent had been physically assaulted within the past school year over gender expression, with 26 percent of the respondents reporting that the physical assault happened "frequently" or "often." Not surprisingly, 83 percent of transgender students and 72 percent of nonbinary gender identifying students reportedly felt unsafe at school.

Intersectionality presents special challenges in matters of bullying. While students were more likely to be harassed and physically assaulted because of gender identity and sexual orientation, they can also experience negativity because of race, religion, and disabilities. Of the respondents, 18 percent reported physical assault within the last year due to religion, 13 percent on account of race or ethnicity, and 10 percent as a result of a disability. Gender nonbinary and transgender students sitting at the identity intersection of racial, ethnic, and/or religious minorities are even more at risk.

Bullying and microaggressions are not acceptable and there are courses of action you can take to address them. First, report any incidents to a trusted teacher or administrator, even those that seem subtle. Invasive questions like "Are you a boy or girl?" or "Do you wear panties or boxers?" are microaggressions and should not be tolerated by you or your school's teachers and administrators. Many instances of bullying are not reported because targeted students feel embarrassed and/or do not trust teachers or administrators. Change starts when victims of bullying come forward. You have the right to feel safe, especially at school.

Cyberbullying

In addition to verbal and physical bullying, gender nonbinary teens are more likely than their cisgender counterparts to become victims of cyberbullying. Cyberbullying is the use of social media, email, blogs, text messages, or other types of technology to harass, threaten, or embarrass other people. In a GLSEN survey, 62 percent of transgender teens experienced some kind of cyberbullying.

Cyberbullying is just as intolerable as verbal or physical bullying. If you or someone you know is experiencing cyberbullying—or you witness cyberbullying of someone you don't know—use these tips to address the situation safely:

- Do not reply. It might be tempting to defend yourself or respond with an equally insulting comment, but this is not a safe way to handle cyberbullying and might make matters worse.

- Do not delete the message. Take a screenshot, print, or forward the message to a trusted adult who can help.
- If an adult doesn't take your concerns seriously, find someone who does.
- Anonymously report any inappropriate posts to forum administrators. If they find your explanation valid, they will remove the post.

If social media causes anxiety, consider unplugging for the time being. Get a little sunshine, read a book, or hang out with friends. Make it a point to do something fun and relaxing.

If you find that you're spending a great deal of time online and are uncomfortable or sad about the things you're seeing, it might be time to change your technology habits. You can set time limits for social media exposure, commit to social media–free zones in your life, and delete or put a hold on your social media platform(s). Social media and other technological advances provide helpful forums with which to stay in touch with distant family, friends, and support groups, but they can also keep you from spending time with important people in your life. Remember to take time to unplug, reflect away from screens, and meet up with your friends for technology-free fun.

Socioeconomic Intersectionality: Gender Nonbinary Teens and Homelessness

Socioeconomic intersectionality plays a large part in the experience of gender-fluid and transgender teens. A gender-fluid teen from a wealthy family in a large urban area is likely to have more support resources—such as finances, support organizations, and public transportation—than someone from an isolated part of the country. This advantage, however, does not guarantee an easier coming-out experience.

A teen's mental health, physical well-being, and economic security often depends on the reaction and level of support offered by loved ones. If a family rejects the teen, it can be devastating and in some cases leads to teen homelessness. They may have to stay with friends or go to a shelter that does not suit their gender or may be unsafe. On the other hand, if parents or guardians embrace and support their nonbinary children's gender identities, the coming-out process can be positive and serve as an inspiration to others.

During the course of the public school bathroom debate in Grass Lake, Michigan, mentioned earlier in this book, Liam's dad, Bill, wrote a supportive and moving essay on what it was like to be the parent of a transgender child. In it, he states:

> *We are always happy to engage in positive discourse and would be happy to answer any questions for people sincerely interested in understanding [gender identity issues]. We have medical staff, parents, and clergy members that would all be willing to lend their expertise and experience … You don't have to believe that our child is a boy. He does. We do. Our doctors do and our families do.*

Sarah Feliciano spends time at a transitional home for homeless LGBTQ+ youth. Forty percent of all homeless youth in the United States identify as LGBTQ+.

Not all gender-fluid and transgender teens have parents as affirming and supportive as Liam's. In many cases, parents kick their gender nonbinary or transgender children out of the house. In other cases, teens are abused at home and run away. A disproportionate number, 40 percent in fact, of all homeless youth in the United States identify as LGBTQ+.

The struggle for resources among the homeless population leads to unsafe and illegal activities. Some teens resort to crime to get money. Others engage in prostitution, where they have sex for money. These practices are dangerous and can lead to prison, sexually transmitted diseases, violence, pregnancy, becoming victims of human trafficking, and death. Supportive families make all the difference to gender-fluid and transgender teens.

10 Great Questions to Ask a School Counselor

1. What would you recommend to students experiencing anxiety about the difference between their assigned gender label and their gender identity?
2. What should I do if I am being bullied in school?
3. If someone comes out as gender-fluid, would you tell their parents?
4. Are there any school or local support groups in the community for gender-fluid teens?
5. What books, magazines, or blogs would you recommend on gender identity issues and gender fluidity?
6. Would you be willing to facilitate a discussion about gender fluidity and gender identity issues in the classroom?

7. What is the school's policy on name changes and the use of pronouns for gender-fluid and transgender students?

8. What is the school's policy on the inclusion of gender-fluid and transgender students on athletic teams?

9. What is the school's policy on transgender students' use of bathrooms and locker rooms that are consistent with their gender identities?

10. If the school does not have policies that are inclusive of gender nonbinary and transgender students, would you please join me in advocating for them?

CHAPTER SIX

Community and Relationships

Sometimes, being gender-fluid, nonbinary, or transgender leads to feelings of isolation. Members of the gender nonbinary community understand this well. For this reason, they are among the most open and receptive communities. They empathize with the struggle to publicly identify as your true self and know the pain of alienation and rejection. If you are feeling alone, you do not have to be. Friends from a remarkably supportive community are waiting for you to reach out to them.

The Gender-Fluid and Transgender Community

There are thousands of organizations and events worldwide for nonbinary and transgender teens

Laverne Cox (*top, center*) advocates to uphold a transgender nondiscrimination law in Massachusetts and is joined in support by local nonbinary individuals.

to connect with one another and celebrate identity. Many groups are easily accessible on social media, including GenderFluid Life and the Gender Fluid Support Network. Groups like these and many others usually publicize resources and local events. The social media landscape changes quickly but a search of #genderfluid on Twitter is also a useful way

Advocates distribute educational material on the Transgender Day of Remembrance (TDOR), November 20. This event honors the lives of those who were murdered in anti-transgender violence.

to connect with the community and plug into the conversation.

When you search for support groups in your area, the local LGBTQ+ community center is a helpful place to start. Such centers are full of useful information on doctors, therapists, legal assistance, and support groups. There are LGBTQ+ support groups in many schools, and online and in-person groups. There are also a number of national organizations through which you can advocate for gender-fluid, nonbinary, and transgender rights. The National Center for Transgender Equality, the Human Rights Campaign, the Trans Youth Equality Foundation, and the Canadian Centre for Gender and Sexual Diversity provide information, resources, and volunteer opportunities to both adults and youth.

The Museum of Trans Hirstory & Art (MOTHA) contributes artistic expression to represent the transgender community. MOTHA's objective is to move "the *hirstory* and art to the center of public life." Prior to the construction of its building, MOTHA is presenting off-site exhibits in North America and throughout the world.

There are Pride events and parades throughout the year, but the month of November brings much-needed public attention to the issues faced by the transgender and gender nonbinary community. Transgender Awareness Month celebrations take place in November, and the Transgender Day of Remembrance (TDOR) is every November 20. TDOR honors the lives of those who were taken in antitransgender violence. It was established in 1999 by transgender advocate Gwendolyn Ann Smith to honor Rita Hester's memory. Rita Hester was an African American transgender woman who was murdered in Allston, Massachusetts, in 1998.

Similarly, March 31 is the International Day of Transgender Visibility. It celebrates the courage it takes to live openly and to raise awareness for transgender issues. In 2009, social worker, licensed psychotherapist, and activist Rachel Crandall (also known as Rachel Crandall-Crocker) founded the International Day of Transgender Visibility to combat the negative portrayal of transgender people in the media. In the years that followed, the day took on a much broader scope of identity celebration and awareness raising.

Dating

Gender-fluid people have choices in dating partners. Some prefer to date cisgender people, while others prefer nonbinary people. Because gender identity and expression do not define the totality of you, consider lots of options to learn what you like. Chances are you will be drawn to others (and others to you) for a vast number of reasons. Explore those reasons and enjoy the process.

With the rise of social media, there are a number of dating apps for transgender and nonbinary people. If you choose to use these, be cautious about what you make public on your profile. Do not publicize any photos, videos, or information that you might later regret. In general, beware of people with poor intentions on dating sites. You do not have to participate in a conversation that makes you feel uncomfortable. Be vigilant of internet predators who give only vague information about themselves and are overly eager to meet you, especially in nonpublic areas.

If you choose to be in a long-term relationship, it is important to remember that there must be mutual respect for the health and well-being of both partners. Rates of relationship abuse and

LGBT Pride Month

In 2009, President Barack Obama declared June as National Lesbian, Gay, Bisexual, Transgender (LGBT) Pride Month. During this time, the nation honors the long-term change that resulted from the 1969 Stonewall riots in Manhattan, a borough of New York City. On the evening of June 27, 1969, police raided the Stonewall Inn and arrested thirteen people. The raid was part of a large, discriminatory crackdown that targeted gay bars for operating without New York State Liquor Authority (SLA) licenses. At that time, SLA refused licenses to bars that served the LGBTQ+ population. Over the six days

(continued on page 88)

In 1969, crowds attempt to prevent police arrests outside the Stonewall Inn. The raid was part of a large, discriminatory crackdown targeting gay bars for operating without licenses.

(continued from page 86)

that followed, people protested the discrimination against the gay community. Hundreds gathered outside the bar chanting, "gay power" and "we want freedom," while others smashed windows and upturned parking meters. Fire hoses were turned on the protestors in response.

Since that time, the Stonewall riots have raised awareness and marked a critical tipping point in the fight for gay rights. Grassroots gay activists hold Gay Pride marches in major cities across the country. Brenda Howard, an American feminist and bisexual rights advocate known as the Mother of Pride, organized the Christopher Street Liberation Day March on the first anniversary of the Stonewall riots. Howard also came up with the idea to commemorate "Pride Day" with a week of events at the end of June. These celebrations became the basis for June as National LGBT Pride Month. Members of the LGBTQ+ community and allies gather to commemorate the freedom they have to be themselves. Pride parades and special events are held in cities all over the world.

sexually transmitted diseases are higher among the transgender population, so it is especially critical to establish your boundaries and be safe if you choose to engage in sexual activities.

Qualities of Allies

It is not necessary for a person to identify as genderfluid to be a respectful, supportive friend to those who are. In fact, cisgender people can be your biggest allies. In her book *Becoming an Ally to the Gender-Expansive Child*, Anna Bianchi explains that the following characteristics are key to being a supportive ally:

- An ally is willing to learn. It is impossible to know what it is like to be another person, but allies will dismiss preconceived notions or stereotypes and they will try to understand you.
- An ally tries to be self-aware. Self-awareness comes to allies as feedback rather than negative criticism of themselves.
- An ally will try to work through personal barriers.
- An ally will stand up for their principles both privately and publicly.

After Catholic University turned down a student request for an LGBT student support group, these empowered allies organized a grassroots group to change the system.

When in search of an ally, look for someone who demonstrates good listening skills, an imagination, empathy, and courage.

It might take some time for those close to you to become allies. You will likely find that some friends and family who had reservations about your gender identity when you first shared it with them will become supportive over time. You might also discover that some family members and friends with whom you thought you could share anything are not supportive, even as time passes. We cannot force others to change their thinking, but it is important for your well-being to recognize who stands as your current and prospective allies. When you do, stay connected with them as much as possible.

If you identify as cisgender, you can be a good ally and friend by being respectful of those who identify as gender nonbinary and transgender, regardless of if you fully understand what they are going through. Refer to gender-fluid and transgender friends by their preferred names and pronouns. If they are being bullied or made fun of behind their backs, stand up for them or notify a trusted adult and serve as their witness. You can support them in using the bathroom or locker room that makes them feel the safest. You also can advocate for gender nonbinary friendly policies like sports inclusion and fair bathroom use. Then take it a step further by joining them in advocacy and celebration efforts in your community.

Taking a Stand with Political Activism

Social expectations for gender norms have come a long way since the 1950s. Society has moved away from the idea that

A gender nonbinary advocate holds a sign that illustrates the evolution of gender norms from the cisgender expectations of the 1950s.

the gender assigned at birth determines one's life course, presentation, and identity. Yet, there is still much to do to reach gender equality for all. This is where advocacy and activism for change can make all the difference.

Consider that the personal is political, meaning that the shaping of hearts and minds does not happen with just policy changes. It begins with personal advocacy and standing up for the right to self-define. It also implies that the definition of gender is based on an internal sense of identity, rather than what society dictates. Activism and advocacy then get to work, making impactful changes to the way people think.

One way to take a stand is in school. Too many transgender and nonbinary students report feeling unsafe at school (83 percent and 72 percent, respectively). Statistics like this indicate a clear inequity for this population, which begins at a young age and worsens in adulthood. Depression and suicide attempts among transgender and gender nonbinary teens are alarmingly high, and substantially higher than those of their cisgender counterparts. If you want to contribute to better outcomes for this population, start by being a friend and ally at school. Advocate for putting an end to bullying, the implementation of fair bathroom use, and inclusion in school athletics. Your example will inspire others, including the adults in your sphere of influence.

Gender-fluid and transgender adults continue to face discrimination. School bullying is often replaced by transphobia among adults. Gender nonbinary and transgender adults also contend with issues of depression and are far more likely to be victims of violence than their cisgender counterparts. They are disproportionately represented among the homeless population and struggle with issues of fair bathroom use, employment, access to medical care, and for US citizens, the right to serve in the US military. Former US vice president Joseph Biden was right to suggest that transgender rights "were the civil rights issue of our time." In social movements, the young usually make the change. You are that change for gender-fluid and transgender individuals.

Glossary

adjudicate To make an official decision to solve a dispute.

apnea A disorder in which breathing repeatedly disrupts sleep.

atrophy The breakdown or wasting away of body tissue or a body part.

cissexism The belief that cisgender people are superior to all others on the gender spectrum.

cyberbullying The use of social media, email, blogs, text messages, or other types of technology to harass, threaten, or embarrass other people.

empirical Describes a finding based on experience or observation, rather than logic or theory.

endocrinology The branch of medicine that focuses on the endocrine glands and hormones.

exacerbates Makes a situation worse.

gender-affirming approach An approach to gender in which a person's internal sense of gender is recognized and respected.

gender expression All of the methods by which people show their gender identity. These might include binding, tucking, hairstyle, clothing, makeup, physical mannerisms, speech patterns, and voice.

gender-variant Behavior or expression that does not conform to masculine or feminine gender norms.

impetus A force that makes something happen.

incongruity Not lining up or fitting with another.

lipid A fat molecule found in living things.

microaggression A subtle verbal or nonverbal insult toward a member of a socially disadvantaged group.

osteoporosis A condition in which one's bones become fragile due to tissue loss.

postgender One who is no longer gendered.

rhetoric The art of persuasive or impressive speaking.

sexual fluidity A change in sexual orientation or desire.

social construct Something that is created or resulting from human interaction, rather than an objective reality.

transgender Relating to one who does not identify with the gender they were assigned at birth.

transphobia Fear and/or discrimination against transgender individuals.

urology The branch of medicine that focuses on the urinary system.

voyeurism The act of gaining sexual pleasure while observing others who are naked or taking part in sexual activities.

For More Information

Canadian Centre for Gender and Sexual Diversity (CCGSD)

440 Albert Street, Suite C304

Albert Street Educational Centre

Ottawa, ON K1R 5B5

Canada

Algonquin Territory

(613) 400-1875

Website: http://ccgsd-ccdgs.org

Facebook: @ccgsd.ccdgs

Instagram and Twitter: @ccgsd_ccdgs

YouTube: CCGSD | CCDGS

Email: info@ccgsd-ccdgs.org

CCGSD supports communities across Canada to assist in providing an environment that is discrimination free for all gender and sexual identities. CCGSD is a leader in the International Day of Pink, encouraging millions of people to wear pink and stand up to bullying.

Gender Diversity

6523 California Avenue SW, #360

Seattle, WA 98136

(855) 443-6337

Website: https://www.genderdiversity.org

Facebook and Twitter: @genderdiversity

Email: info@genderdiversity.org

Gender Diversity raises awareness and understanding of gender diversity by providing educational resources and increasing societal awareness.

Gender Management Service (GeMS) at Boston Children's Hospital

333 Longwood Avenue, Second Floor

Boston, MA 02115

(617) 355-4367

Website: http://www.childrenshospital.org/centers-and-services/programs/f-_-n/gender-management-service

Facebook: @BostonChildrensHospital

Instagram: @bostonchildrens

Twitter: @BostonChildrens

YouTube: Boston Children's Hospital

Boston Children's treats patients up to age twenty-one, offering a wide range of health care services. GeMS is committed to providing the highest level of individualized, safe, and affirmative care for gender-expansive and transgender children, teens, and young adults.

Gender Spectrum

(510) 788-4412

Website: https://www.genderspectrum.org

Facebook and Twitter: @GenderSpectrum

YouTube: Gender Spectrum

Email: info@genderspectrum.org

Gender Spectrum provides educational resources to help create inclusive and gender-sensitive environments for children and teens.

GLSEN (formerly known as the Gay and Lesbian Independent School Teachers Network)

110 William Street, 30th Floor

New York, NY 10038

(212) 727-0135

Website: https://www.glsen.org/learn/about-glsen

Facebook, Twitter, and YouTube: @GLSEN

Email: info@glsen.org

GLSEN provides resources to create safe and affirming schools for people of all gender identities and sexual orientations.

National Center for Transgender Equality (NCTE)

1133 19th Street NW, Suite 302

Washington, DC 20036

(202) 642-4542

Website: http://transequality.org

Facebook: @TransEqualityNow

Twitter: @TransEquality

YouTube: National Center for Transgender Equality

Email: ncte@transequality.org

NCTE advocates for social justice and equality for transgender people by providing information and lobbying for policy change.

Trans Equality Society of Alberta

PO Box 2053 Edmonton Main

Edmonton, AB T5J 2P4

Canada

Website: http://www.tesaonline.org

Facebook: Trans Equality Society of Alberta

Twitter: @TESAonlineorg

Email: info@tesaonline.org

Trans Equality Society of Alberta provides educational resources and advocates for social justice and equality for transgender people in Alberta and throughout Canada.

Transgender Legal Defense and Education Fund (TLDEF)

20 West 20th Street, Suite 705

New York, NY 10011

(646) 862-9396

Website: http://transgenderlegal.org

Facebook: @TransLegalDefense

Twitter: @TLDEF

Email: info@transgenderlegal.org

TLDEF is committed to ending discrimination and achieving equality for all transgender people through the provision of educational resources and legal counsel. It provides pro bono legal name change services and has adjudicated transgender rights cases in the areas of employment, health care, education, and public accommodations.

Trans Youth Equality Foundation (TYEF)

PO Box 7441

Portland, ME 04112-7441

(207) 478-4087

Website: http://www.transyouthequality.org

Facebook: @transyouthequality

Instagram: @transyouthequalityfoundation

Twitter: @TYEFofficial

Tumblr: http://transyouthequality.tumblr.com

Blog: http://www.transyouthequality.org/tyef-blog

Email: contact@transyouthequality.org

TYEF advocates for transgender, gender nonbinary, and intersex youth. Founded by the mother of a transgender child, TYEF seeks to provide high-quality resources and support services for children and their families.

The Trevor Project

PO Box 69232

West Hollywood, CA 90069

West Hollywood Office: (310) 271-8845

New York Office: (212) 695-8650

Crisis Line: (866) 488-7386

TrevorText: Text "START" to 678678

Website: https://www.thetrevorproject.org

Facebook: @TheTrevorProject

Instagram: @trevorproject

Twitter: @TrevorProject

Email: info@thetrevorproject.org

The Trevor Project is a nonprofit organization that offers educational resources and provides 24/7 crisis and suicide intervention to lesbian, gay, bisexual, transgender, and questioning people under twenty-five.

True Colors Fund

330 West 38th Street, Suite 405

New York, NY 10018

(212) 461-4401

Website: https://truecolorsfund.org

Facebook: @truecolorsfund

Twitter: @TrueColorsFund

True Colors Fund works to prevent and end homelessness among LGBTQ+ youth, as well as to create a world where each individual can be themselves.

For Further Reading

Adams, Gloria. *Coping with Sexism and Misogyny.* New York, NY: Rosen YA, 2018.

Fisher, Owl, and Fox Fisher. *Trans Teen Survival Guide.* London, UK, and Philadelphia, PA: Jessica Kingsley Publishers, 2019.

Garvin, Jeff. *Symptoms of Being Human.* New York, NY: Balzer & Bray, 2016.

Hines, Sally. *Is Gender Fluid? A Primer for the 21st Century.* New York, NY, and London, UK: Thames & Hudson, 2018.

Hurt, Avery. *Coping with Hate and Intolerance.* New York, NY: Rosen YA, 2018.

Jennings, Jazz. *Being Jazz: My Life as a Transgender Teen.* New York, NY: Ember, 2016.

Kuklin, Susan. *Beyond Magenta: Transgender Teens Speak Out.* Somerville, MA: Candlewick, 2014.

McGrody, Ellen. *Coping with Gender Dysphoria.* New York, NY: Rosen YA, 2018.

Testa, Rylan J., Deborah Coolhart, and Jayme Peta. *The Gender Quest Workbook: A Guide to Teens & Young Adults Exploring Gender Identity.* Oakland, CA: Instant Help, 2015.

Woods, Sara. *Identifying as Transgender.* New York, NY: Rosen YA, 2017.

Bibliography

Barnett, Brian. "Anti-Trans Bathroom Bills Are Based on Lies." *Huffington Post*, September 11, 2018. https://www.huffingtonpost.com/entry/opinion-transgender-bathroom-crime_us_5b96c5b0e4b0511db3e52825.

Butler, Judith. *Gender Trouble: Feminism and the Subversion of Identity.* New York, NY: Routledge, 1990.

Centers for Disease Control and Prevention. "Transgender Identity and Experiences of Violence Victimization, Substance Use, Suicide Risk, and Sexual Risk Behaviors Among High School Students," Morbidity and Mortality Weekly Report 68, no. 3: 67–71 (January 25, 2019). https://www.cdc.gov/mmwr/volumes/68/wr/mm6803a3.htm?s_cid=mm6803a3_w.

Chicago Legal Forum 1989 no. 1 (Article 8). Chicago, IL: University of Chicago Legal Forum, 1989. https://chicagounbound.uchicago.edu/cgi/viewcontent.cgi?article=1052&context=uclf.

Crenshaw, Kimberlé. "Demarginalizing the Intersection of Race and Sex: A Black Feminist Critique of Antidiscrimination Doctrine, Feminist Theory and Antiracist Politics." University of Chicago Legal Forum. Retrieved May 21, 2019. https://philpapers.org/rec/CREDTI.

Ford, Zack. "Michigan Mom Defends Her Trans Kid Against a Hostile Town." ThinkProgress, September 22, 2017. https://thinkprogress.org/grass-lake-transgender-school-78559a70d44a.

GLSEN. "Harsh Realities: The Experience of Transgender Youth in Our Nation's Schools." Retrieved January 28, 2019. https://www.glsen.org/sites/default/files/Harsh%20Realities.pdf.

GLSEN. "Trans Inclusion in High School Athletics." Retrieved January 21, 2019. https://www.glsen.org.

Hancox, Lewis. "My Top 8 Tips on Coming Out as Trans." Ditch the Label, April 20, 2018. https://us.ditchthelabel.org/8-tips-for-coming-out-as-trans.

Hayes-Skelton, Sarah, and David Pantalone. "Anxiety and Depression in Sexual Minority Individuals." Anxiety and Depression Association of America. Retrieved January 28, 2019. https://adaa.org/sexual-gender-minority-individuals.

Human Rights Campaign Foundation. "A National Epidemic: Fatal Anti-Transgender Violence in America in 2018." Retrieved January 25, 2019. https://assets2.hrc.org/files/assets/resources/AntiTransViolence-2018Report-Final.pdf?_ga=2.266395662.1423057933.1548288029-1805272765.1548288029.

James, Herman, Keisling Rankin, and Anafi Mottet. *The Report of the 2015 U.S. Transgender Survey*. Washington, DC: National Center for Transgender Equality, 2016. https://www.transequality.org/sites/default/files/docs/USTS-Full-Report-FINAL.PDF.

Keisling, Mara. "Celebrating 15 Years." Medium, January 6, 2018. https://medium.com/transequalitynow/celebrating-15-years-d98b9278c434.

Liam, transgender teen, and parents, Jaimie and Bill, interview and email exchanges with the author, January 2019.

Liptak, Adam. "Supreme Court Revives Transgender Ban for Military Service." *New York Times*, January 22, 2019. https://www.nytimes.com/2019/01/22/us/politics/transgender-ban-military-supreme-court.html.

Marsh, Sarah. "The Gender-Fluid Generation: Young People on Being Male, Female or Non-Binary." *Guardian*, March 23, 2016. https://www.theguardian.com/commentisfree/2016/mar/23/gender-fluid-generation-young-people-male-female-trans.

Mayo Clinic Staff. "Depression." Retrieved January 28, 2019. https://www.mayoclinic.org/diseases-conditions /depression/symptoms-causes/syc-20356007.

McGreal, Chris. "Interview: Rachel Dolezal." *Guardian*, December 13, 2015. https://www.theguardian.com /us-news/2015/dec/13/rachel-dolezal-i-wasnt-identifying -as-black-to-upset-people-i-was-being-me.

National Center for Biotechnology Information. "Gender Dysphoria in Adolescence: Current Perspectives." NCBI, March 2, 2018. https://www.ncbi.nlm.nih.gov/pmc/articles /PMC5841333/#b11-ahmt-9-031.

Rider, G. Nicole, Barbara McMorris, Amy L. Gower, Eli Coleman, and Marla E. Eisenberg. "Health and Care Utilization of Transgender and Gender Nonconforming Youth: A Population-Based Study." *Pediatrics* 141, no. 3 (March 2018). http://pediatrics.aappublications.org /content/141/3/e20171683.

Tarnished Sophia, blog. "Wrong Body, Right Mind: Living with Gender Dysphoria." June 13, 2013. https://tarnishedsophia .wordpress.com/2013/06/16/wrong-body-right-mind -living-with-gender-dysphoria.

Vanity Fair. "The Crucifixion of Matthew Shepard." March 1999. https://www.vanityfair.com/news/1999/13/matthew -shepard-199903.

WPATH. *Standards of Care for the Health of Transsexual, Transgender, and Gender Nonconforming People*. The World Professional Association for Transgender Health. Retrieved January 30, 2019. https://www.wpath.org/media/cms /Documents/Web%20Transfer/SOC/Standards%20of%20 Care%20V7%20-%202011%20WPATH.pdf.

Index

S

T

V

W

About the Author

Stephanie Lundquist-Arora has master's degrees in political science and public administration, with a special focus in gender and politics, as well as gender theory more broadly. She helped to organize and facilitate Amnesty International London's Gender and Refugee Conference while interning with Amnesty International's Women's Officer. She also assisted in teaching an undergraduate-level gender and politics course at Syracuse University. When not writing, Lundquist-Arora likes traveling with her family, jogging, learning jiu-jitsu, reading, and trying new foods.

Photo Credits

Cover, pp. 32–33 Adam Hester/Getty Images; p. 6 Emma McIntyre/Getty Images; p. 9 Nick Dolding/Stone/Getty Images; p. 11 H. Armstrong Roberts/ClassicStock/Archive Photos/Getty Images; pp. 13, 29 Library of Congress Prints and Photographs; p. 14 Keystone/Hulton Archive/Getty Images; p. 16 © AP Images; p. 21 Drew Angerer/Getty Images; p. 22 Steve Liss/The LIFE Images Collection/Getty Images; p. 26 Icon Sportswire/Getty Images; p. 37 Everett Collection Inc./Alamy Live News/Alamy; p. 40 Sara D. Davis/Getty Images; p. 44 Cindy Ord/Getty Images; pp. 46–47 U.S. Navy photo by Mass Communication Specialist 3rd Class Patrick Semales; p. 51 fizkes/Shutterstock.com; p. 54 Kansas City Star/Tribune News Service/Getty Images; pp. 58, 76–77, 90-91 The Washington Post/Getty Images; p. 62 KatarzynaBialasiewicz/iStock/Getty Images; p. 65 Spencer Platt/Getty Images; p. 66 Neilson Barnard/Getty Images; p. 68 Estrada Anton/Shutterstock.com; p. 73 Geoff du Feu/Photographer's Choice/Getty Images; p. 81 Natasha Moustache/Getty Images; pp. 82–83 Diana Mrazikova/VWPics/Newscom; pp. 86–87 New York Daily News Archive/Getty Images; pp. 92–93 Stefan Holm/Shutterstock.com.

Design: Michael Moy; Layout and Photo Researcher: Ellina Litmanovich; Editor: Erin Staley